Animal Neighbours

Deer

Michael Leach

WAYLAND

Animal Neighbours

Titles in this series:

Badger • Deer • Fox • Hare • Hedgehog • Otter

Conceived and produced for Hodder Wayland by

Nutshell
MEDIA

Intergen House, 65–67 Western Road, Hove BN3 2JQ, UK
www.nutshellmedialtd.co.uk

Commissioning Editor: Vicky Brooker
Designer: Tim Mayer
Illustrator: Jackie Harland
Picture Research: Glass Onion Pictures

Published in Great Britain in 2003 by Hodder Wayland, an imprint of Hodder Children's Books.

This paperback edition published in 2007 by Wayland, an imprint of Hachette Children's Books.

British Library Cataloguing in Publication Data
Leach, Michael, 1954–
Deer. – (Animal neighbours)
1. Deers – Juvenile literature
I. Title
599.6'5

ISBN-13: 978 0 7502 5086 3

Printed and bound in China.

Wayland,
an imprint of Hachette Children's Books
338 Euston Road, London NW1 3BH

Cover photograph: A male roe deer licks a new shoot of conifer before taking a bite.
Title page: A stag is caught eating a flower it has just stolen from a garden.

Picture acknowledgements
FLPA 6 (Minden Pictures), 12 (Michael Clark), 15 (Walter Rohdich), 17 (Derek Middleton), 26 (John Watkins); Michael Leach 20, 28 top left; Nature Picture Library 10 (Adrian Davies), 27 (Staffan Widstrand); NHPA *Cover, Title page* (Manfred Danegger), 7 (Helio & Van Ingen), 9 (Manfred Danegger), 11 (Gerard Lacz), 13 (Laurie Campbell), 18 (Andy Rouse), 19 (Manfred Danegger), 21 (Henry Ausloos), 24, 25, 28 right (Manfred Danegger), 28 bottom (Gerard Lacz); Oxford Scientific Films 8 (Peter Weimann), 14 (Mike Birkhead), 22 (Hans Reinhard/OKAPIA), 23 (Daniel Cox), 28 top (Peter Weimann).

Contents

Meet the Deer

Deer are hoofed mammals with long, thin legs. The males of most species have antlers on their heads. They live in woodlands, forests and grasslands.

There are 36 species of deer alive today living throughout the world. This book looks at the roe deer, the most common deer in Europe and Asia.

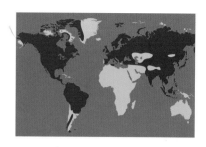

▲ The red areas of this map show where deer live in the world today.

Coat

The roe deer's coat is perfect camouflage amongst woodlands and forests.

Tail

A short tail is hidden beneath a white patch of hair. When alarmed or aggressive, this hair is puffed out as a signal to other deer.

Legs

Long, thin legs make the deer a fast runner.

DEER FACTS

The roe deer's scientific name is *Capreolus capreolus*, from the Latin word *capreolus*, meaning 'little goat'.

Males are known as stags, bucks or bulls, females as does, hinds or cows, new-born deer as kids or fawns, and young deer as calves.

Roe deer are about 110 cm long and weigh between 18–29 kg.

A roe stag. ▲

4

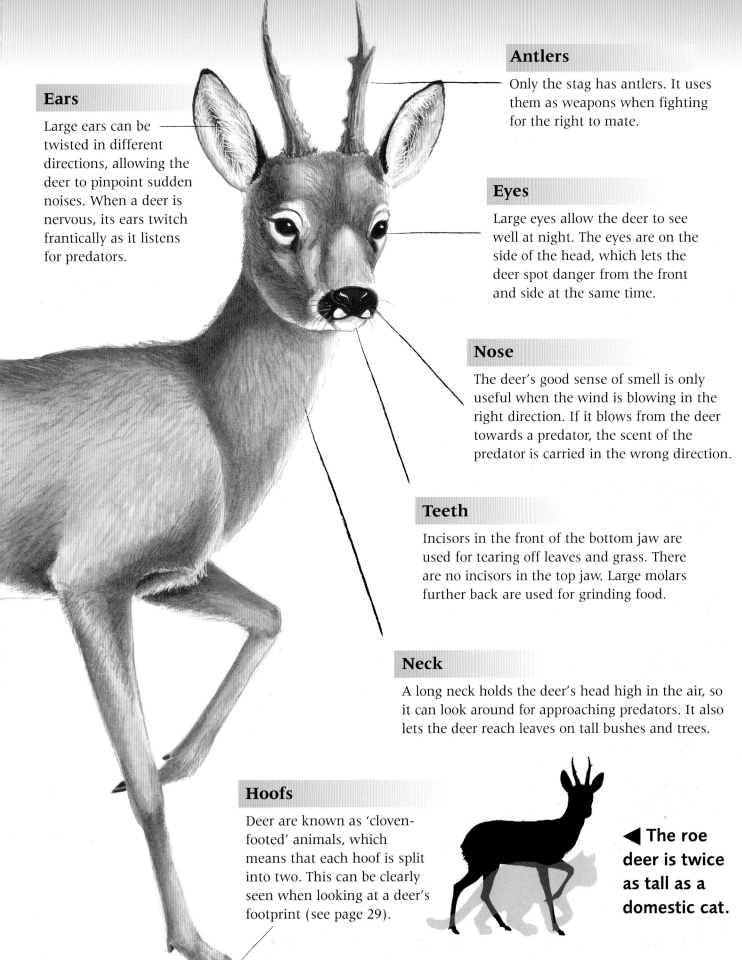

Ears

Large ears can be twisted in different directions, allowing the deer to pinpoint sudden noises. When a deer is nervous, its ears twitch frantically as it listens for predators.

Antlers

Only the stag has antlers. It uses them as weapons when fighting for the right to mate.

Eyes

Large eyes allow the deer to see well at night. The eyes are on the side of the head, which lets the deer spot danger from the front and side at the same time.

Nose

The deer's good sense of smell is only useful when the wind is blowing in the right direction. If it blows from the deer towards a predator, the scent of the predator is carried in the wrong direction.

Teeth

Incisors in the front of the bottom jaw are used for tearing off leaves and grass. There are no incisors in the top jaw. Large molars further back are used for grinding food.

Neck

A long neck holds the deer's head high in the air, so it can look around for approaching predators. It also lets the deer reach leaves on tall bushes and trees.

Hoofs

Deer are known as 'cloven-footed' animals, which means that each hoof is split into two. This can be clearly seen when looking at a deer's footprint (see page 29).

◄ **The roe deer is twice as tall as a domestic cat.**

The Deer Family

Deer belong to a huge family known as the ungulates. All ungulates have hoofed feet. The family contains nearly 190 species, including pigs, horses, camels and giraffes. Hoofs are made of keratin, the same substance that forms human fingernails.

◄ Elk (or moose) spend most of the summer feeding on plants growing just under the surface of lakes and rivers.

BIGGEST AND SMALLEST

The largest deer is the elk, which lives in Europe, North America, and Asia. In North America it is known as the moose. It measures 2.3 m high at the shoulder and can weigh up to 800 kg. The smallest deer is the southern pudu, from South America, which is just 38 cm high and weighs 8 kg.

▼ Reindeer live in herds of up to 10,000 animals.

Some species of deer are specially adapted to their habitat. Reindeer live in the open spaces of the Arctic, where there are few trees to hide them from wolves and other large predators. To help protect each other, the reindeer live in huge herds. Every animal is alert for danger and can warn the others if a predator appears.

Deer that live in herds, such as reindeer, usually have the largest antlers because the stags must fight for territory and females. Deer that live alone, such as roe deer, rarely need to fight, so they have smaller antlers. Water deer and musk deer are the only species that have no antlers at all.

Birth and Growing Up

It is early June, and a pregnant doe looks for a hidden place to give birth, away from the prying eyes of predators. Giving birth is very dangerous for a doe because the scent of her new-born kid might attract a hungry predator.

▼ This new-born kid is still wobbly on its feet. A kid's muscles are very weak for the first few hours of life, but they quickly grow stronger.

The kid is born covered in fur with its eyes open. After a few minutes it struggles to find its feet, wobbling for a moment or two before collapsing. But it soon learns to balance, and within 30 minutes of being born the kid can walk. By then it probably has a twin, and the two kids find their feet together. By the end of the day, the kids are able to run.

KIDS

New-born roe kids are about 25 cm long and weigh about 1.7 kg.

A doe normally gives birth to twins, but she can have between one and three kids.

▲ The kid's spotted coat is very different to the reddish-brown colour of its mother.

Immediately after the birth, the mother licks her kids all over. This allows both mother and young to learn each other's scent. Now they will be able to recognise each other by smell alone.

For their first few weeks, roe deer kids stay hidden amongst the vegetation while their mother goes off to feed. They are not fast enough to follow their mother, so they stay in one spot and wait for her to return to them several times a day, when they suckle her milk.

Early days

The first few days of a kid's life are the most dangerous. Many are killed by foxes, eagles or other predators. At first, they stay in one place, keeping very still and silent as they hide amongst the undergrowth. After a few days they start to move short distances, but they always stay close to the spot where they were born. Their dappled coat helps to camouflage them, hiding them from enemy eyes.

Roe kids first begin eating leaves at the age of about 2 weeks, copying their mother as she tears them off branches. But they still rely on their mother's milk for food. When they are between 6 and 8 weeks old the young deer, who are now called calves, join their mother and learn to eat the same food as the adults.

▲ The kid's dappled coat makes it very difficult to see on the woodland floor.

ORPHAN KIDS?

It is easy to think that kids lying alone in the undergrowth have been abandoned by their mother, but she will simply have gone off to feed. If you find a kid, it is very important not to touch it. Deer hate the scent of humans. If a doe returns to find human scent on her kid, she will not allow it to suckle and the young deer will die of starvation.

As the calves grow, their coat slowly changes to a smooth, reddish-brown, the same colour as the adults. They spend a lot of time playing amongst themselves, taking it in turns to chase each other and play-fight. This exercise strengthens the calves' leg muscles and improves the speed of their reactions, so it is excellent practise for avoiding predators.

▼ Calves can soon run fast enough to keep up with their mother and avoid most predators.

Habitat

When they reach the age of about 10 months, it is time for young deer to leave their mother and find their own territory. The roe deer's favourite habitat is woodland. Its reddish-brown coat is perfect camouflage amongst the thick undergrowth. In winter, its coat turns grey to reflect the changing colours of its surroundings, as trees lose their leaves and dawn frost covers the ground.

▼ Roe deer often raid parks and gardens to look for food, but after eating they return to the safety of woodland.

Over the last 500 years, many woodlands have been cut down to create more farmland, and towns have spread into the surrounding countryside. Roe deer have had to learn to adapt to the areas left to them. Many continue to use woods as shelter in the daytime, but come out at night to feed in fields, gardens and parks. Their small size and shy behaviour means that they can live close to humans without being seen very often.

This roe deer is well ▶ camouflaged amongst the shadows of a mature forest.

DEER HUNTING

For several centuries, European kings kept large areas of forest as their own private deer-hunting grounds. In the eleventh century, in Britain, William the Conqueror passed the Forest Law to protect his deer. Anyone found killing deer would be hung, and poachers that tried to kill deer but failed would have both hands cut off. The penalty for even disturbing a deer would be to have both eyes taken out.

Territory

Roe deer usually live alone, or in small groups. Each deer or group of deer has its own feeding range, or territory. Young does usually make their territory close to their mother's range, but young stags must travel further away when they become independent.

During the breeding season, stags become very defensive of their territory. Each stag marks its territory by rubbing its antlers up and down tree bark. It will also leave urine on bushes and the leaves of short trees, which is known as scent-marking.

Eating and sleeping

Roe deer feed throughout the night, but they are most active around dusk and dawn. They spend most days sleeping in a quiet, sheltered spot. The shelter hides them from predators and stops them overheating in the hot summer sun. In winter, when food is harder to find, deer will also eat during the day.

DEER CALLS

Stags bark like a dog to attract does and warn off rivals. Does sometimes use soft bleats to call their young. The rest of the time, deer are usually silent.

▼ Roe deer are extremely good at leaping. They often jump streams and hedges to escape from predators.

Food

Deer are herbivores, which means they eat only plants. They eat a wide variety of vegetation, including grass, leaves, twigs, flowers, seeds and fruit. Plants do not contain much nutrition, so deer must eat a lot of food to get the nourishment they need.

▼ Adult deer are too fast for most predators, but kids are hunted by foxes and birds of prey. (The illustrations are not to scale.)

Deer food chain

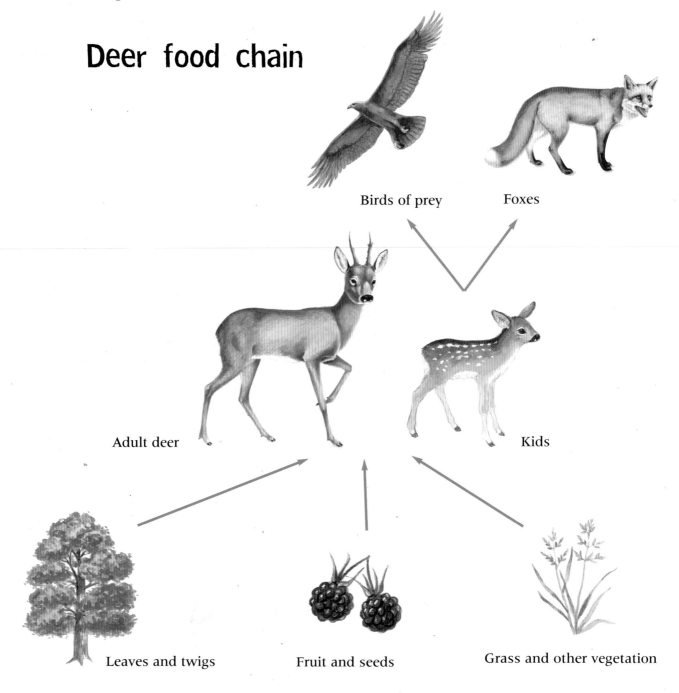

Birds of prey

Foxes

Adult deer

Kids

Leaves and twigs

Fruit and seeds

Grass and other vegetation

▲ Autumn nuts that fall from trees are rich in protein.

EATING

Deer have two different ways of feeding: grazing and browsing. They graze by eating plants such as grass, which grow on the ground. They browse by eating leaves and other food that is found on bushes and trees.

While they feed, deer regularly stop and look around for enemies. Even when asleep, a deer's ears and nose are constantly alert for signs of danger. If they hear a sudden sound or detect a strange scent, they spring instantly to their feet.

The roe deer's diet changes slightly throughout the year, depending on the food available. In the summer, they eat the leaves of trees such as oak and hazel. In autumn, they take advantage of the huge supply of nuts and fruits, particularly acorns. In the winter, when deciduous trees lose their leaves, the deer eat evergreens such as ivy, heather, ferns and pine needles.

Chewing the cud

Deer do not thoroughly chew their food immediately. They eat as much as they can at once and then chew it properly later. They bite off parts of a plant with their sharp incisor teeth, cut it up with one or two strokes of the large molar teeth at the back of the mouth and then swallow. The food travels down to the deer's stomach.

▲ When deer learn to feed on crops, they can become pests to farmers.

The stomach of a deer is divided into four chambers. Fresh food is stored in the first of these chambers. When this is full, the deer brings the food back into its mouth and chews it thoroughly again before swallowing. This time the food enters the second stomach chamber, before passing through the rest of the digestive system. This is known as 'chewing the cud'. Animals that have a four-chambered stomach, including deer, cattle and sheep, are called ruminants.

TEETH

Deer have eight sharp incisor teeth in their lower jaw, but instead of front teeth in their upper jaw they have a thick, hard pad of flesh. When eating, the deer rips off food between the bottom teeth and the pad of flesh in its top gum. Further back in the mouth there are large, flat molars and premolars for chewing.

◄ In the spring and summer, roe deer often browse on the tender new shoots of young trees.

Finding a Mate

After the age of 14 months, does are ready to breed. Stags are also old enough to breed at this age, but often they must wait another few years before they are strong enough to fight off other stags and defend their own territory.

Roe deer breed just once a year, during the breeding season. This is known as the rut, or rutting season, and it is between July and August each year.

▼ Roe stags need to be in perfect condition at the start of the breeding season if they are to have a chance of mating.

During the rut, stags fight each other for the right to mate. They bark and chase each other in circles, trying to drive off the other stag. Then they charge at each other and lock antlers, pushing and twisting in a test of strength. Eventually the strongest, or dominant, stag wins. He will mate with every doe inside his territory. After mating, the stag plays no part in rearing the kids.

▲ Red deer stags have bigger antlers than those of roe deer. Their stag fights can end in death for the loser.

Antlers

Deer are the only animals that have antlers, and apart from reindeer, they only grow on the stags. Antlers are made of the same substance as bone, and they grow incredibly fast. In just four months, a roe stag grows a pair of antlers that are 30 centimetres long and weigh 600 grams. The antlers fall off between November and January every year, but a new pair is fully grown by March.

▼ Dead velvet shrivels and falls off in early spring. Stags sometimes rub their antlers against branches to remove the last scraps of velvet.

New antlers first appear as tiny bumps on top of the stag's head. At first, they are covered with a soft skin, known as velvet. This contains blood vessels that supply nutrition to the growing antlers. When the antlers reach full size, by the end of March, the velvet dies and drops off, revealing the new antlers beneath.

▲ **Dropped antlers are soon eaten by mice or other animals.**

ANTLER FEAST

When antlers fall off, they are nibbled and chewed by other animals such as mice, rats and even deer themselves. Antlers are a good source of minerals including calcium, which all animals need for strong bone growth. In Far Eastern countries such as China, deer antlers are an ingredient in local medicines. They are cut up and dried, then ground into a powder and added to drinks believed to cure headaches and blindness.

Roe deer and other species of deer living in thick woodland have much smaller antlers than species living in more open habitats. This prevents the antlers being tangled in the thick vegetation. The roe deer's antlers measure about 25 centimetres at their widest point compared to the antlers of the moose, which can measure up to 2 metres wide.

Threats

Roe deer can live for up to 14 years in the wild, but most die before the age of 8. Healthy adult deer outrun most predators, but young or weak deer are often caught and eaten because they are not fast enough to get away. Up to 50 per cent of roe kids and calves are killed by foxes, owls and birds of prey every year.

◀ This European eagle owl has killed a kid.

ENDANGERED SPECIES

The roe deer and many other species have high populations, but other deer species are threatened by extinction. Fea's muntjac lives in Thailand and is so rare that it has only been seen a few times over the past ten years. Pere David's deer originally lived in China, but today it is completely unknown in the wild and only exists in zoos.

As more and more roads are built through deer habitats, the number of deer killed by traffic each year increases. Deer can cause serious road accidents, so they can be a great danger to drivers. In many countries, road builders must find out about deer in an area before building a new road through it.

Older deer learn to keep away from traffic. Some will graze on grass verges and completely ignore noisy cars passing just a few metres away. But if a vehicle stops and a person climbs out, the deer will immediately run off.

▼ At dusk, it can be difficult to see a deer crossing the road. Road traffic is one of the roe deer's biggest threats.

Hunting and culling

▲ People still hunt
deer for sport with
specially trained dogs.

People have hunted the roe deer for meat since the
Stone Age. Deer meat is known as venison and it was
an important food in the past. Although wild deer are
still hunted for meat, most venison now comes from
commercial deer farms. However, deer are still
hunted for sport in many countries and their meat
is used for food.

When there are too many deer in one area, they can damage forestry, farm crops and people's gardens. Large numbers of deer can also mean that many starve to death because there is not enough food available. To protect the deer's environment, other animals that share their habitat and the deer themselves, deer are sometimes culled, or killed. Culling usually means being killed by shooting, to cause as little pain as possible.

▼ This deer has been culled to reduce the number of deer in the area.

REINDEER

The Lapp people of northern Scandinavia used to base their entire lives on reindeer. They relied on the deer for food and used their skin for clothes, following the herds as they migrated from winter to summer feeding areas. Some Lapps still make their living from reindeer, but most now work in fishing or other jobs.

Deer Life Cycle

1 The new-born kid has its eyes open and is covered in fur.

2 The kid relies on its mother's milk until it is between 6 and 8 weeks old.

3 For its first 6 or 7 weeks, the kid stays hidden in the undergrowth while its mother goes out to feed.

4 At 6 or 7 weeks old, the kid joins its mother and follows her as she feeds.

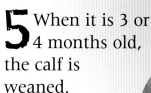

5 When it is 3 or 4 months old, the calf is weaned.

6 At 18 months old, stags' antlers start to grow and females are ready to breed.

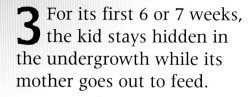

Deer Clues

Look out for the following clues to help you find signs of a deer:

Footprints
Roe deer footprints are clearly divided into two. They can easily be confused with sheep tracks. Roe deer tracks are narrower than those of sheep, and the two halves are closer together.

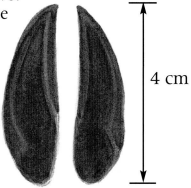

4 cm

Hair
Deer hair is thick and straight. Look for tufts caught on twigs and fences.

Dropped antlers
Roe stags drop their antlers between November and January every year. Different species of deer have their own size and design of antlers, so it is possible to tell the species of deer from the antlers.

Deer calls
At night, in the rutting season, stags bark like a dog to attract does and warn off rivals.

Flattened vegetation
Deer sleeping during the day leave large areas of flattened grass and vegetation. These are usually in cool, sheltered places, away from the heat of the midday sun.

Droppings
Deer droppings are smooth, black and oval.

10–14 mm

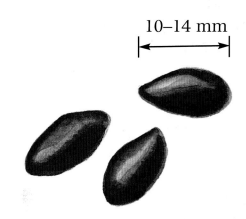

Frayed undergrowth
During the rutting season, stags sweep their antlers through trees and plants as part of their display, leaving them torn and ragged.

Peeled tree bark
Peeled areas of tree trunk can be a sign that a deer is close by. Deer often use their sharp incisors to bite tree bark. Teeth marks on tree trunks also act as signals to other deer, warning them that the territory is already taken.

Glossary

antlers The two bony growths on top of a deer's head.

birds of prey Birds that hunt animals for food.

browsing Eating leaves from bushes or trees.

camouflage The colour or pattern of an animal that helps it blend in with its surroundings and makes it hard to see.

deciduous A tree that sheds all its leaves in the autumn.

doe A female deer.

dominant The largest, strongest animal of the group.

evergreens Trees or shrubs that have leaves all year round.

extinction Dying out.

grazing Eating plants, mainly grass, which grow low down on the ground.

herbivore An animal that eats just plant food.

incisors Sharp teeth at the front of the mouth, used for cutting and slicing.

migrate To move from one place to live in another.

molars Large, flat teeth at the back of the mouth, used for chewing and grinding.

predator An animal that eats other animals.

premolars Large, flat teeth at the back of the mouth, just in front of the molars, used for chewing and grinding.

stag A male deer.

Stone Age A period of time over 8,000 years ago when people used tools made from stone.

suckle When a mother allows her young to drink milk from her teats.

territory The area that is defended and controlled by an animal.

velvet The soft layer of skin that covers growing antlers.

weaned A young mammal is weaned when it stops taking milk from its mother and eats only solid food.

Finding Out More

Other books to read

All About Deer by Jim Arnosky (Scholastic, 1999)

Animals in Order: Camels and Pigs: What have they in common? by Erin Pembrey Swan (Watts, 1999)

Animal Sanctuary by John Bryant (Open Gate Press, 1999)

Animal Young: Mammals by Rod Theodorou (Heinemann, 2000)

Classification: Animal Kingdom by Kate Whyman (Wayland, 2000)

Deer by Norma Chapman (Whittet Books, 1999)

Deer Watching by Diane Bair and Pamela Wright (Capstone Press, 2000)

The Giant Book of Creatures of the Night by Jim Pipe (Watts, 1998)

Life Cycles: Cats and Other Mammals by Sally Morgan (Chrysalis, 2003)

Naturebooks: Deer by Mary Berendes (Child's World Inc, 1999)

New Encyclopedia of Mammals by David Macdonald (OUP, 2001)

Reading About Mammals by Anna Claybourne (Watts, 2000)

The Wayland Book of Common British Mammals by Shirley Thompson (Wayland, 1998)

What's the Difference?: Mammals by Stephen Savage (Wayland, 2002)

Wild Britain: Woodlands by R. & L. Spilsbury (Heinemann, 2002)

Zoobooks: Deer Family by Timothy L. Biel (Wildlife Education Ltd, 1997)

Organisations to contact

The British Deer Society
Tel. 01425 655434
www.bds.org.uk
A charity devoted to the welfare of deer.

Countryside Foundation for Education
PO Box 8, Hebden Bridge HX7 5YJ
www.countrysidefoundation.org.uk
Training and teaching materials to promote the understanding of the countryside and its problems.

English Nature
Northminster House, Peterborough, Cambridgeshire PE1 1UA
Tel. 01733 455100
www.english-nature.org.uk

The Mammal Society
2B Inworth Street,
London SW11 3EP
www.abdn.ac.uk/mammal/
Promotes the study and conservation of British mammals.

Wildlife Watch
National Office, The Kiln, Waterside, Mather Road, Newark NG24 1WT
www.wildlifetrusts.org.uk
Junior branch of the Wildlife Trusts, a network of local Wildlife Trusts caring for nearly 2,500 nature reserves, from rugged coastline to urban wildlife havens, protecting a huge number of habitats and species.

Index

Page numbers in **bold** refer to a photograph or illustration.